Tessellation Winners
Escher-like original student art
The First Contest

1990 Contest Winners

Grades 1–2: Audrea Ramirez

Grades 3–4: Karen Kalb

Grades 5–6: Jason Phan

Grades 7–8: Lydia Payne

Grades 9–10: Ryan Cooper

Grades 11–Up: Paul O'Hearn

DALE SEYMOUR PUBLICATIONS

Cover tessellation by Stephanie Wilson

Grateful acknowledgment is made to Cordon Art in Baarn, Holland, exclusive worldwide representatives of the M. C. Escher heirs, for permission to reproduce the design of M. C. Escher on page 79.

Order number DS21108
ISBN 0-86651-548-8

3 4 5 6 7 8 9 10-MA-96 95 94

**DALE
SEYMOUR
PUBLICATIONS**
P.O. BOX 10888
PALO ALTO, CA 94303

Contents

Preface

During the 1989–1990 school year, Dale Seymour Publications sponsored a contest inviting students to create original, Escher-like tessellations. By the contest deadline—June 30, 1990—we had received more than 1200 entries from students as young as first grade to students in high school and beyond.

Tessellation Winners is a compilation of the top student designs from the contest, grouped in these divisions: grades 1–2, 3–4, 5–6, 7–8, 9–10, and 11 and up. In each division, the overall winner's tessellation appears first, followed by the designs of the honorable mention winners. The book concludes with a brief overview of techniques for generating tessellating patterns, a bibliography of resources, and the announcement and rules for our next contest.

Selecting the winners presented a fascinating challenge! Because we received only a few entries from the early grades, hundreds from the middle grades, and a moderate number from secondary students, we determined that not all the divisions should have the same number of winners. So, the number of honorable mention winners varies from division to division. The winners represent a wide variety of striking images that are characteristic of the entries from each group.

Some of the factors we considered when reviewing the entries include

- care taken by the student to create a true tessellating pattern,
- techniques used by the student to generate the shapes,
- originality of the design (inspired by Escher, but not an imitation of existing Escher designs), and
- artistic appeal of the final drawing.

Readers looking for a more comprehensive study of tessellations may be interested in the book that launched this contest, *Introduction to Tessellations*, by Dale Seymour and Jill Britton (Palo Alto, CA: Dale Seymour Publications, 1989). This resource book, from which our brief overview of techniques is drawn, fully explores the fundamental concepts of tessellations.

We hope you enjoy *Tessellation Winners!* We wish to thank all those students and teachers who submitted tessellations, and we hope this book inspires others to explore these intriguing geometric designs.

For information about the next contest, turn to page 99. Since we've made a few changes from the first contest, please check the new procedures for submitting entries. In particular, we've added a new category for teachers. Note that the deadline for entries is June 30, 1992—so entries from school year 1990–1991 or 1991–1992 are eligible.

The Winning Artists

Stephanie Wilson
Cover Artist

Audrea Ramirez
1–2 Winner

Karen Kalb
3–4 Winner

Jason Phan
5–6 Winner

Lydia Payne
7–8 Winner

Ryan Cooper
9–10 Winner

Paul O'Hearn
11–Up Winner

Grades 1–2

Winner

Audrea Ramirez

Honorable Mention

Danny Bedwell

Antwoine Harrington

Jack Hennessey

Lindsay Ray

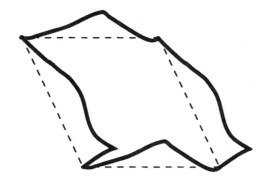

Audrea Ramirez

Grade: 1

Spring Mill Elementary School

Indianapolis, Indiana

Teachers: Jolee Garris and Pat Ward

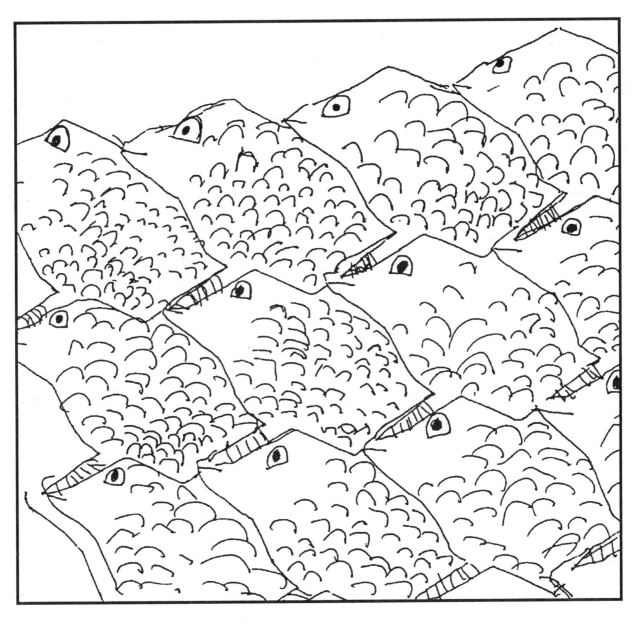

Danny Bedwell

Grade: 1

Spring Mill Elementary School

Indianapolis, Indiana

Teachers: Jolee Garris and Pat Ward

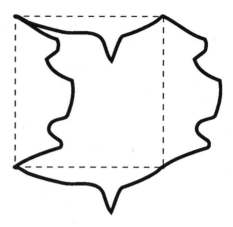

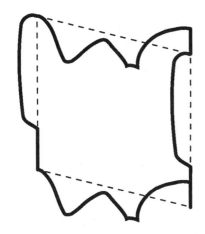

Antwoine Harrington

Grade: 1

Spring Mill Elementary School

Indianapolis, Indiana

Teachers: Jolee Garris and Pat Ward

Jack Hennessey

Grade: 1

Spring Mill Elementary School

Indianapolis, Indiana

Teachers: Jolee Garris and Pat Ward

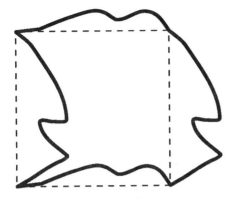

Lindsay Ray

Grade: 1

Spring Mill Elementary School

Indianapolis, Indiana

Teachers: Jolee Garris and Pat Ward

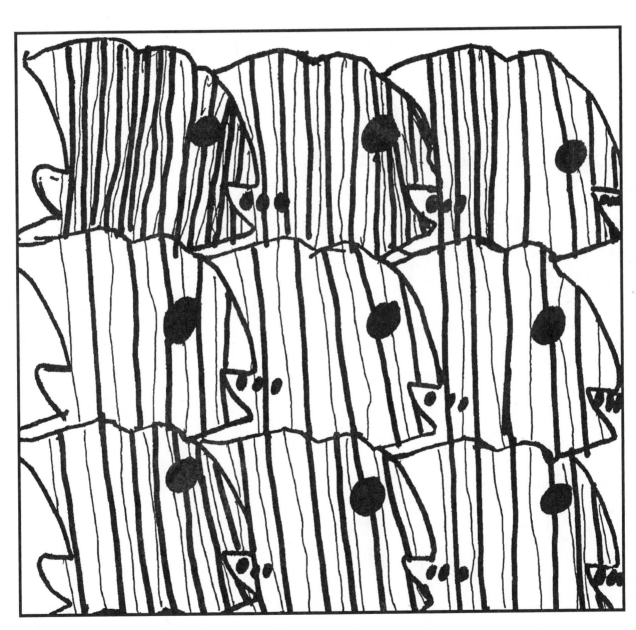

Grades 3–4

Winner

Karen Kalb

Honorable Mention

Karmen Cassell

Craig Erdrich

Chris Hogue

Bryan Lins

Kenny Mize

Sarah Reisner

Tiffany Winters

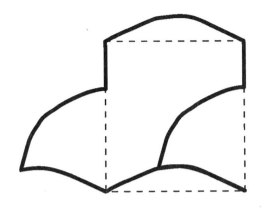

Karen Kalb

Grade: 4

Kimberlin Academy for Excellence

Garland, Texas

Teacher: Kathy Jordan

Karmen Cassell

Grade: 4

Effie Green Elementary School

Raleigh, North Carolina

Teacher: Carolyn Jo Johnson

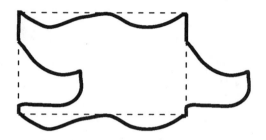

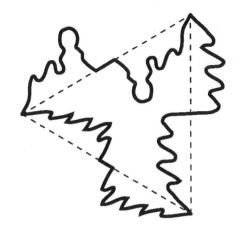

Craig Erdrich

Grade: 3

Mill Creek Towne Elementary School

Rockville, Maryland

Teacher: Marilyn Graber

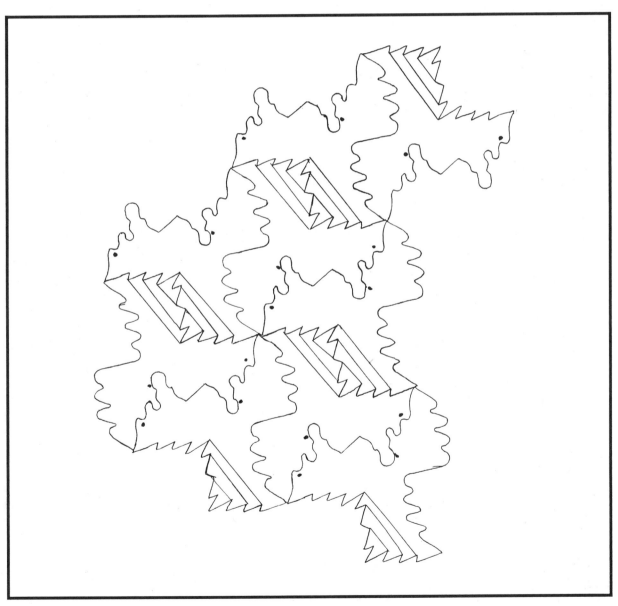

Chris Hogue

Grade: 3

Emerson Elementary Language Arts and
    Computer Magnet School

Westerville, Ohio

Teacher: Linda Lagemann

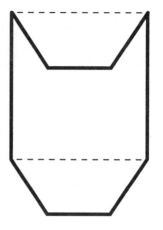

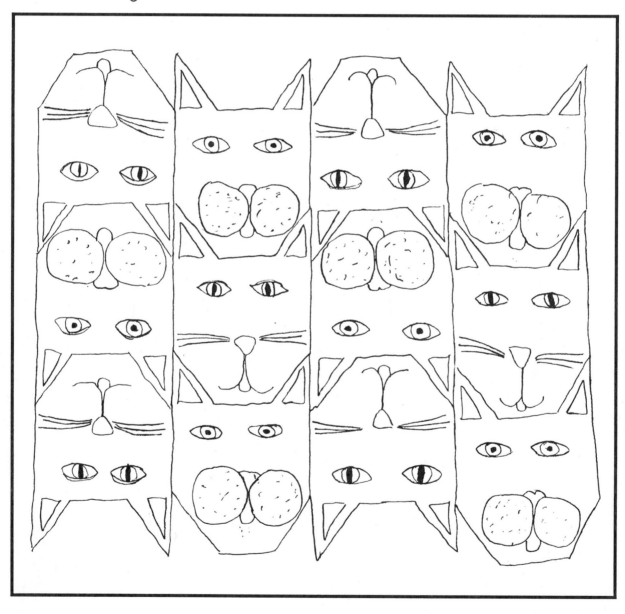

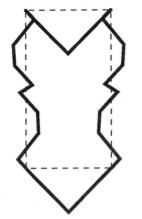

Bryan Lins

Grade: 4

Kimberlin Academy for Excellence

Garland, Texas

Teacher: Kathy Jordan

Kenny Mize

Grade: 4

Stone School

Saginaw, Michigan

Teacher: Judy Sizelove

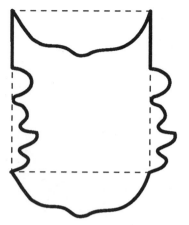

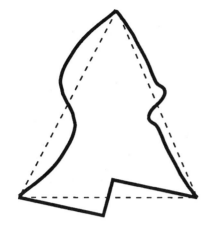

Sarah Reisner

Grade: 3

Litchfield Elementary School

Litchfield, Ohio

Teacher: Esther Kucinski

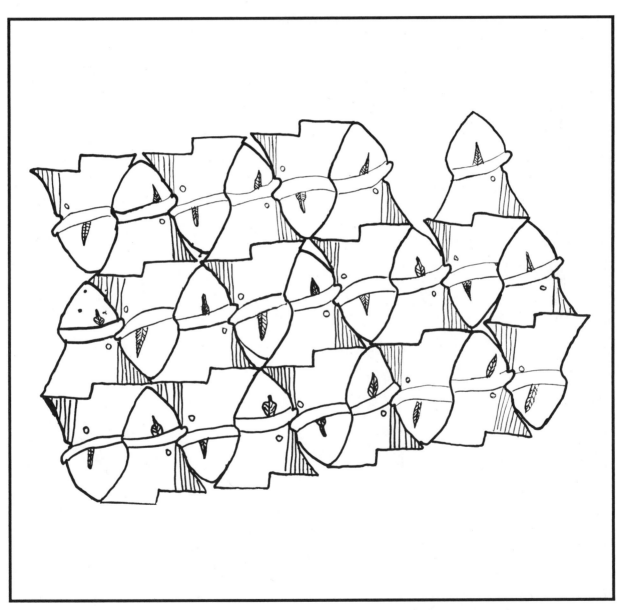

Tiffany Winters

Grade: 4

Effie Green Elementary School

Raleigh, North Carolina

Teacher: Carolyn Jo Johnson

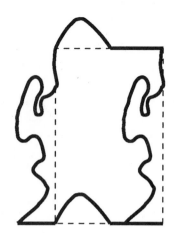

Grades 5–6

Winner

Jason Phan

Honorable Mention

Jason Abele

Gretchen Bohl

Jenny Buchanan

Becca Hafer

Susan Kibrick

Natalie Lester

Kevin Dale Lewis

Kelly Neyland

John Petzinger

Joe Spence

John Wylie

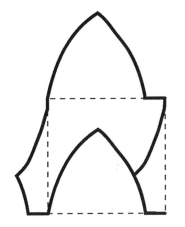

Jason Phan

Grade: 5

Kimberlin Academy for Excellence

Garland, Texas

Teacher: Sally Timms

Jason Abele

Grade: 5

High Point Elementary School

Gahanna, Ohio

Teacher: Penny Ellsworth

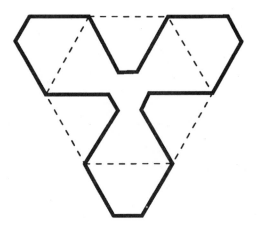

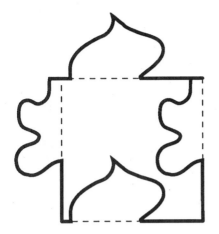

Gretchen Bohl

Grade: 6
Montrose Elementary School
Columbus, Ohio
Teacher: Becky Liefeld

Jenny Buchanan

Grade: 5

Kimberlin Academy for Excellence

Garland, Texas

Teacher: Sally Timms

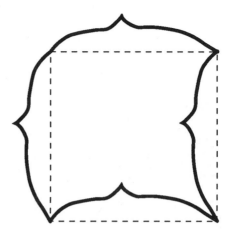

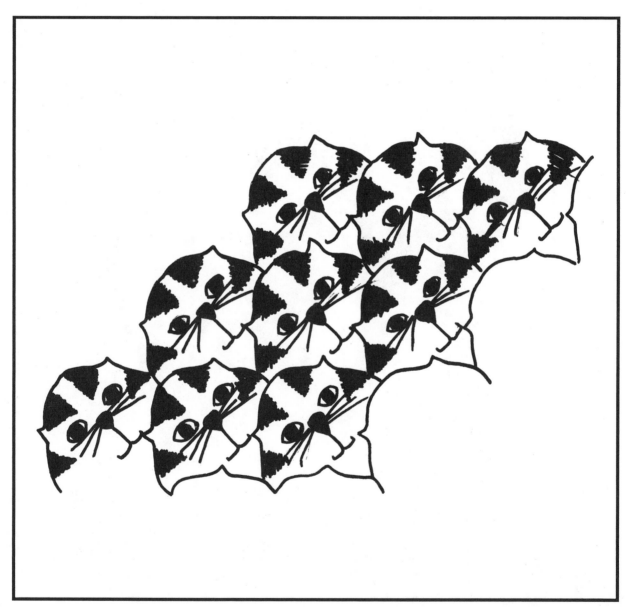

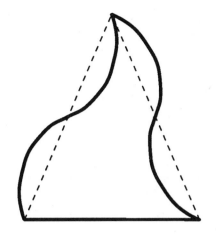

Becca Hafer

Grade: 5

Litchfield Elementary School

Litchfield, Ohio

Teacher: Esther Kucinski

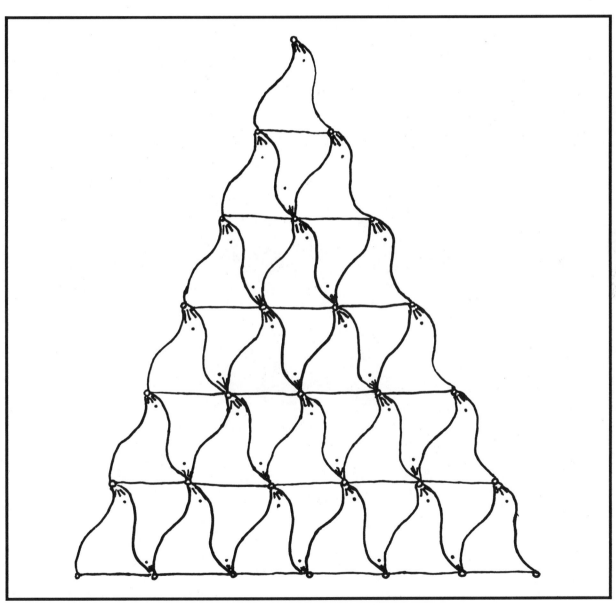

Susan Kibrick

Grade: 5

Open School Magnet

Los Angeles, California

Teacher: Mona Lynne Sheppard

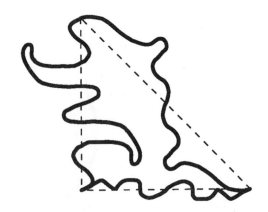

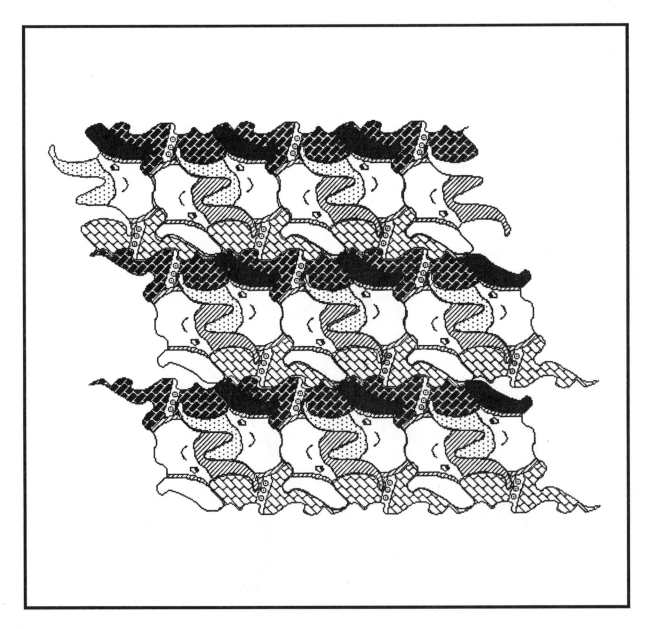

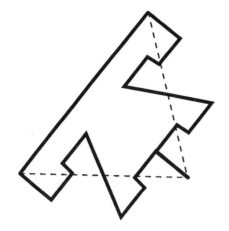

Natalie Lester

Grade: 5
High Point Elementary School
Gahanna, Ohio
Teacher: Penny Ellsworth

Kevin Dale Lewis

Grade: 6

Open School Magnet

Los Angeles, California

Teacher: Mona Lynne Sheppard

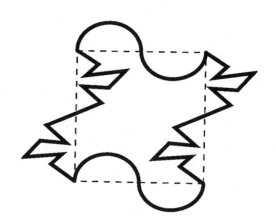

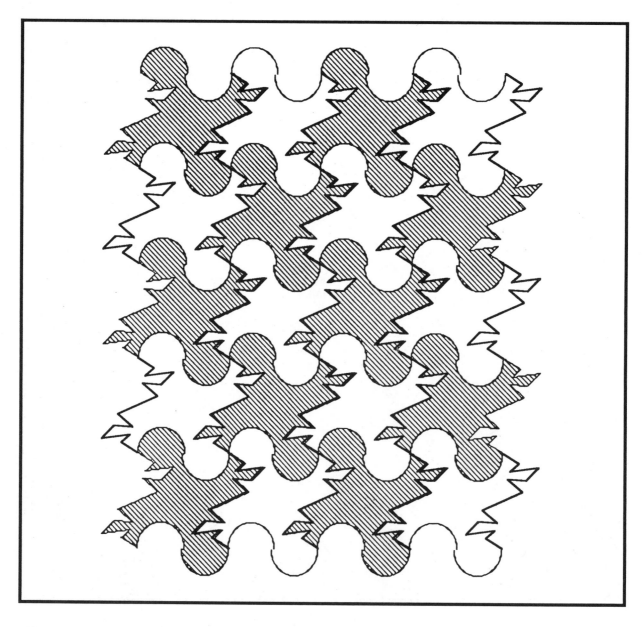

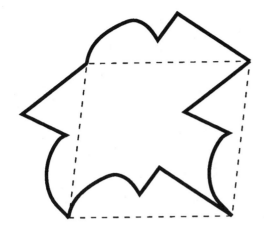

Kelly Neyland

Grade: 6
Fulton Elementary School
Toledo, Ohio

John Petzinger

Grade: 6

Montrose Elementary School

Columbus, Ohio

Teacher: Becky Liefeld

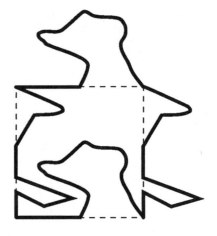

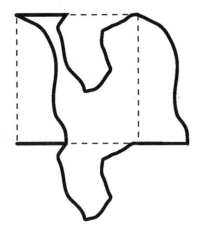

Joe Spence

Grade: 6

Montrose Elementary School

Columbus, Ohio

Teacher: Becky Liefeld

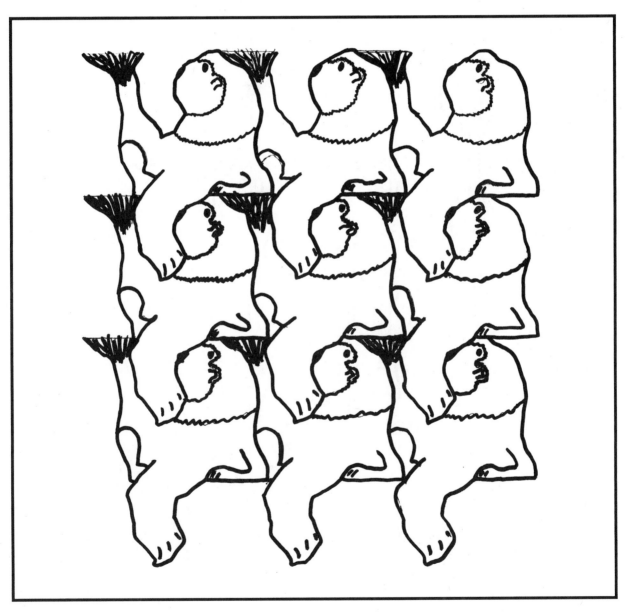

John Wylie

Grade: 6

Granby Elementary School

Columbus, Ohio

Teacher: Penny Ury

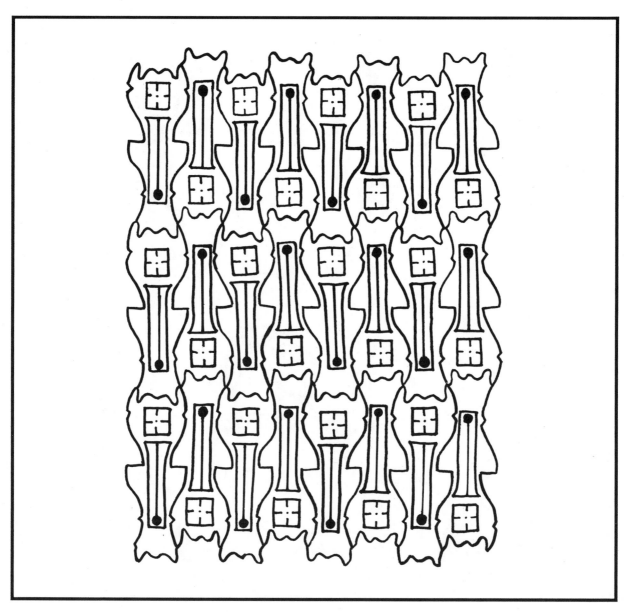

Grades 7–8

Winner

Lydia Payne

Honorable Mention

Chuck Aubrey

Christine Chang

Elisabeth Enenbach

Theo Honohan

Mandi Johnson

Luis Lopez

Heather McCoy

Aaron Nauman

Conrad R. Pack

Jill Petras

Summer Rawleigh

Josh Richards

Lydia Payne

Grade: 8

La Loma Junior High School

Modesto, California

Teacher: Nancy Breckenridge

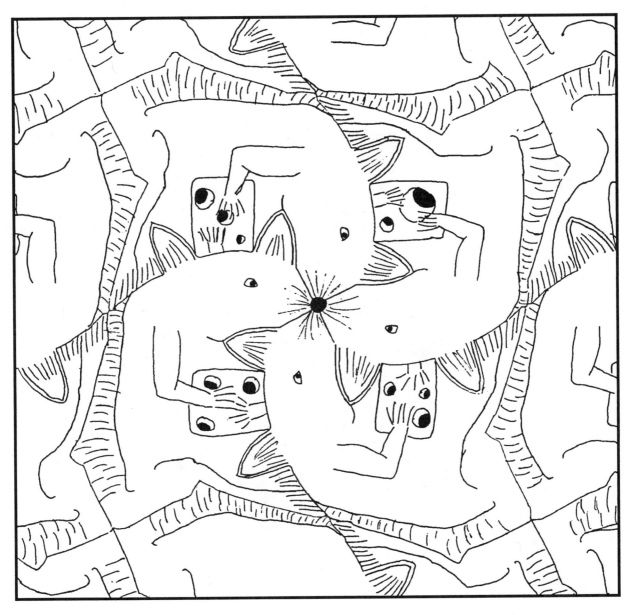

Chuck Aubrey

Grade: 7

Heritage Middle School

Columbus, Ohio

Teacher: Laurel Tair Pettit

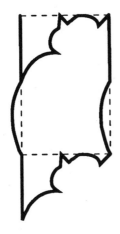

7–8 Honorable Mention

Christine Chang

Grade: 8

Malaga Cove Intermediate School

Palos Verdes Estates, California

Teacher: Beverly Mairs

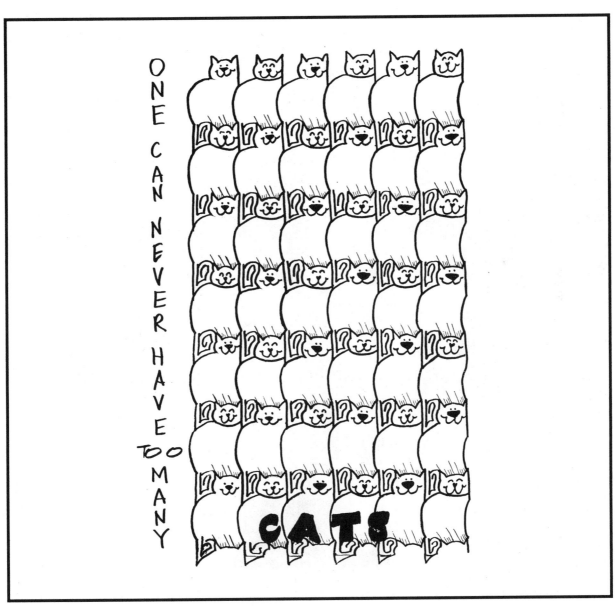

Elisabeth Enenbach

Grade: 7

Tuttle Middle School

Crawfordsville, Indiana

Teacher: Dean Swalley

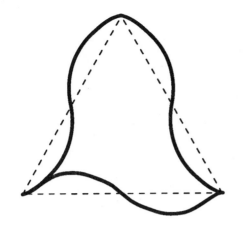

Theo Honohan

Grade: 7

Sheridan School

Washington, District of Columbia

Teacher: Shirley Hughes

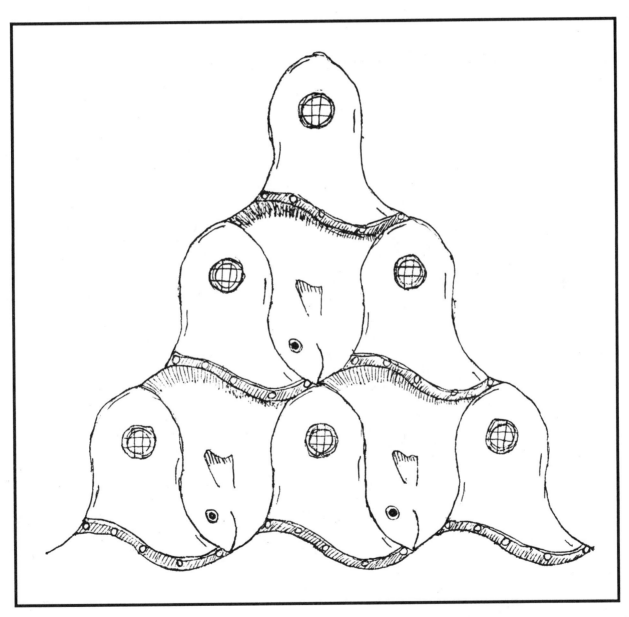

Mandi Johnson

Grade: 7

Madison Junior High School

Rexburg, Idaho

Teacher: Karen Klingler

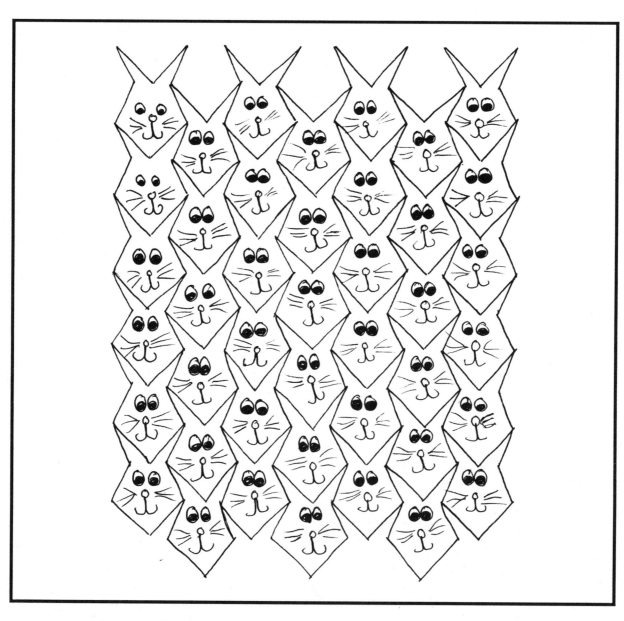

Luis Lopez

Grade: 7

Prarie Middle School

Aurora, Colorado

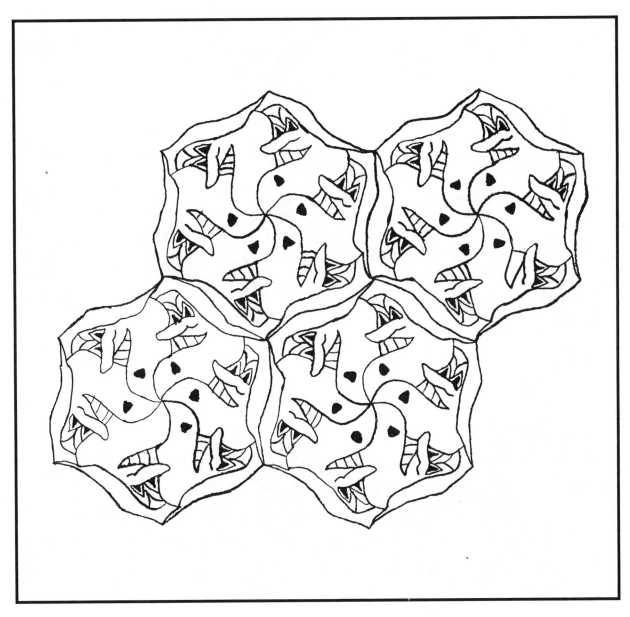

Heather McCoy

Grade: 8

Indiana Area Junior High School

Indiana, Pennsylvania

Teacher: Susan Soughry

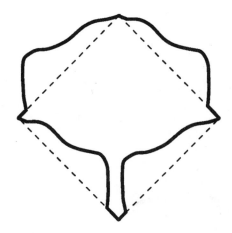

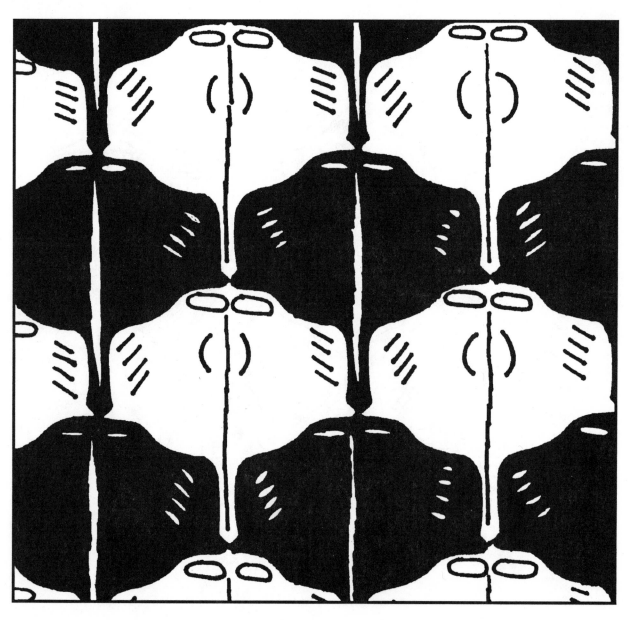

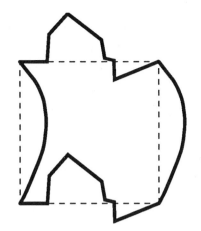

Aaron Nauman

Grade: 7

Heritage Middle School

Columbus, Ohio

Teacher: Laurel Tair Pettit

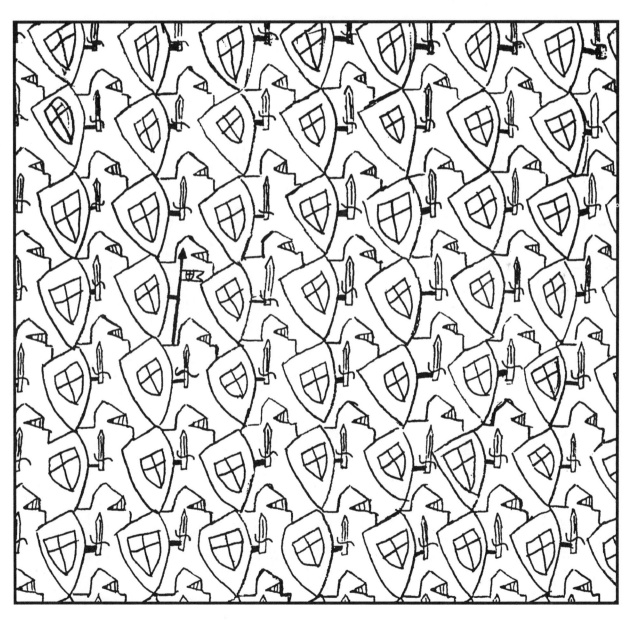

Conrad R. Pack

Grade: 7

Madison Junior High School

Rexburg, Idaho

Teacher: Karen Klingler

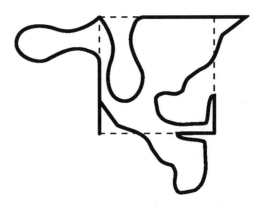

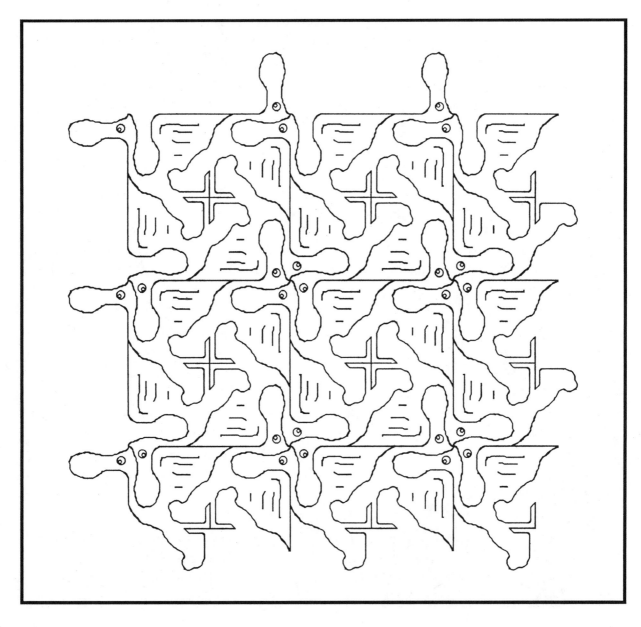

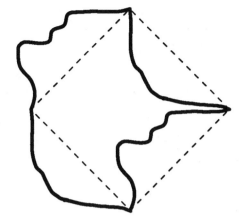

Jill Petras

Grade: 8

Indiana Area Junior High School

Indiana, Pennsylvania

Teacher: Susan Soughry

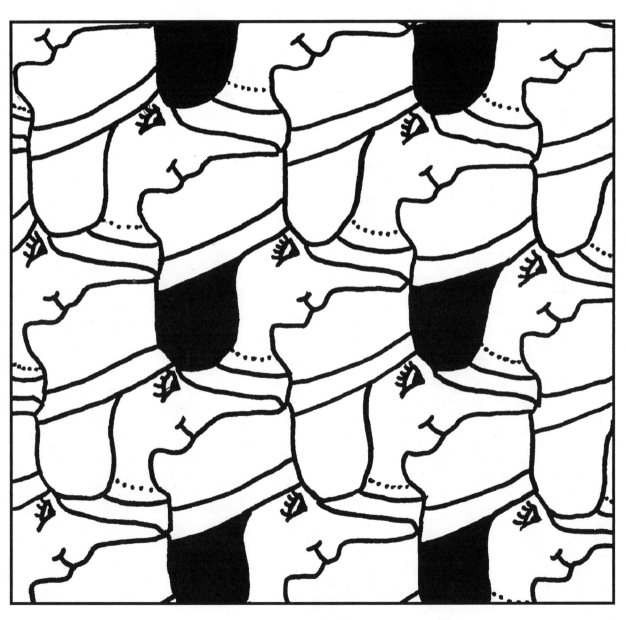

Summer Rawleigh

Grade: 8

La Loma Junior High School

Modesto, California

Teacher: Nancy Breckenridge

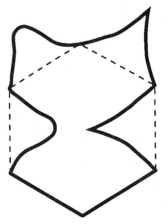

Josh Richards

Grade: 8

Indiana Area Junior High School

Indiana, Pennsylvania

Teacher: Susan Soughry

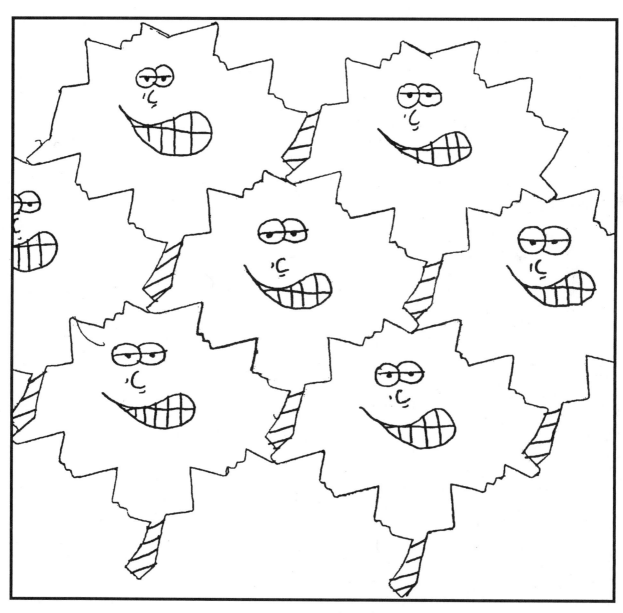

Grades 9–10

Winner
Ryan Cooper

Honorable Mention
Matt Anderson

Terry Frame

Liz Hall

Gretchen Hilliard

Sandy Lee

Danny Palovick

Roz Pirozzi

Kristie Silvius

Ian Oakley Smith

Fred Thaete

Stephanie Wilson

Alicia Wong

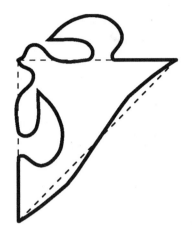

Ryan Cooper

Grade: 10
Marion High School
Marion, Illinois
Teacher: Catherine Howell

Matt Anderson

Grade: 9

Eagle Rock Junior High School

Idaho Falls, Idaho

Teacher: Linda Borrenpohl

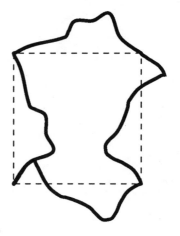

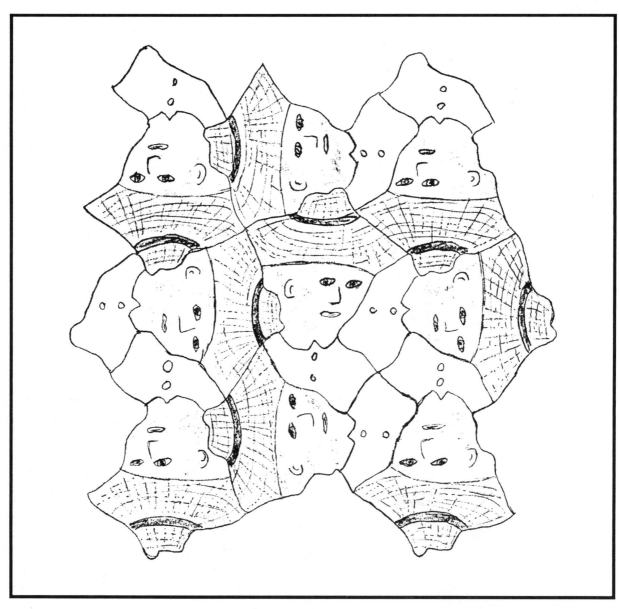

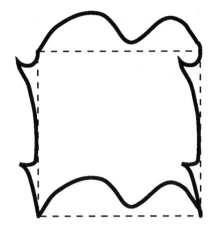

Terry Frame

Grade: 10

Zanesville High School

Zanesville, Ohio

Teacher: Margaret A. Garner

Liz Hall

Grade: 10

McLean High School

McLean, Virginia

Teacher: Joan Gifford

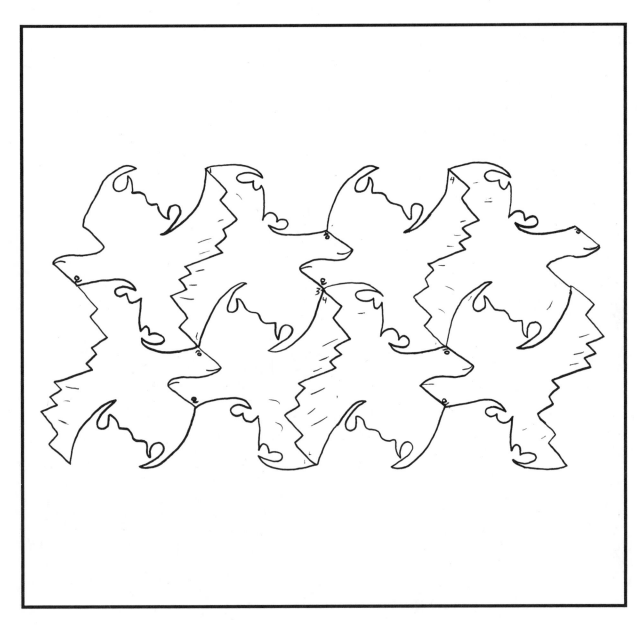

Gretchen Hilliard

Grade: 10

Marion High School

Marion, Illinois

Teacher: Catherine Howell

Sandy Lee

Grade: 9

El Toro High School

El Toro, California

Teacher: Cheryl O'Malley

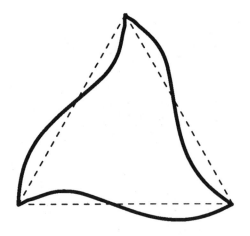

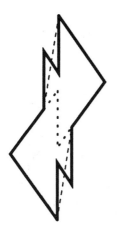

Danny Palovick

Grade: 10

Marion High School

Marion, Illinois

Teacher: Catherine Howell

Roz Pirozzi

Grade: 10

Pinkerton Academy

Derry, New Hampshire

Teacher: Nancy Fletcher

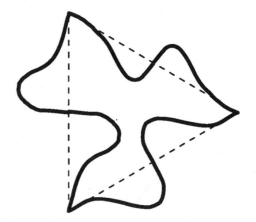

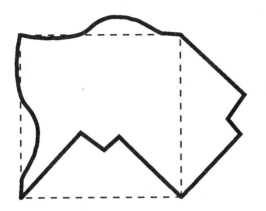

Kristie Silvius

Grade: 10

Marion High School

Marion, Illinois

Teacher: Catherine Howell

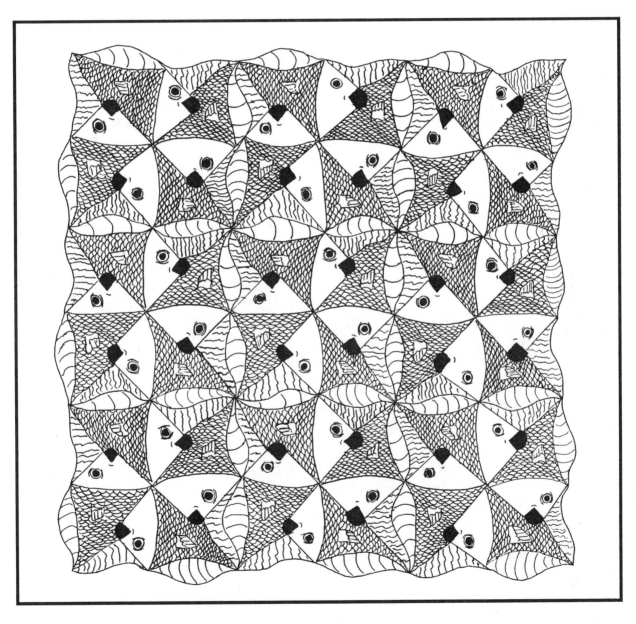

Ian Oakley Smith

Grade: 10

North Hollywod High School Highly Gifted Magnet

North Hollywod, California

Teacher: Gail Grande

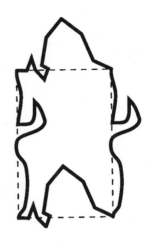

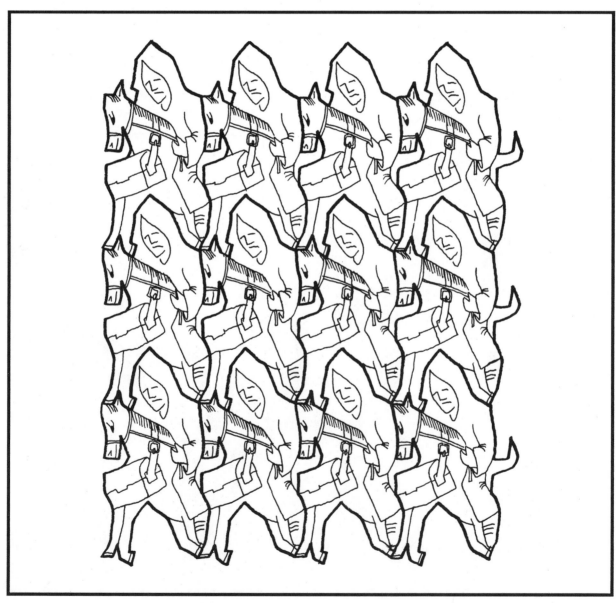

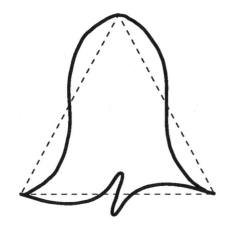

Fred Thaete

Grade: 9

Shawnee Mission Northwest High School

Shawnee Mission, Kansas

Teacher: Martha Teitze

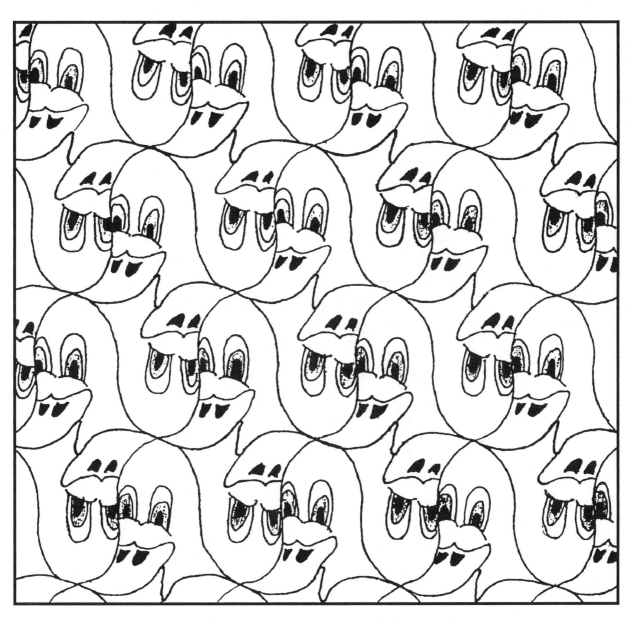

Stephanie Wilson

Grade: 10

North Hollywood High School

North Hollywod, California

Teacher: Gail Grande

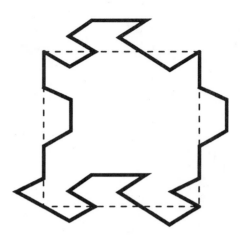

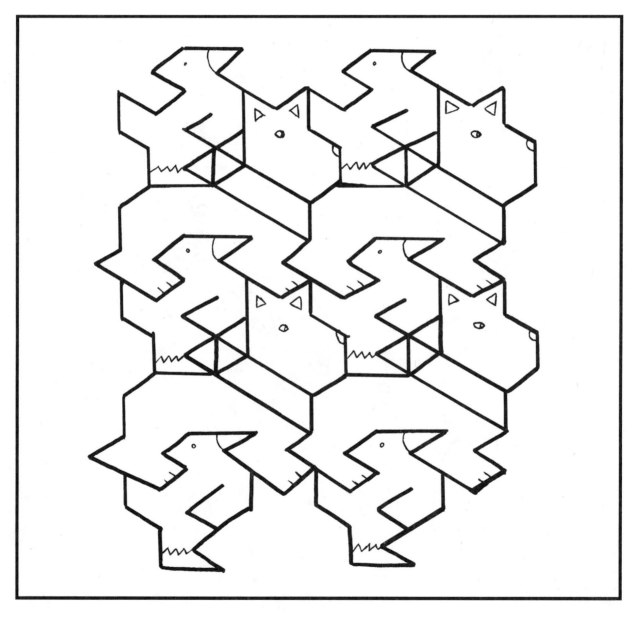

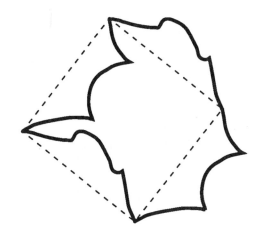

Alicia Wong

Grade: 9

Tennyson High School

Hayward, California

Teacher: Oran Pyle

Grades 11–Up

Winner
Paul O'Hearn

Honorable Mention
Todd Adamson

Robin Allred

Jonathan Bunch

Amy B. Caldwell

Donnie Cook

Tom Marcille

Edward R. Mears

Britta Peterson

Steve Richmond

Steve Sawyer

Derek Squire

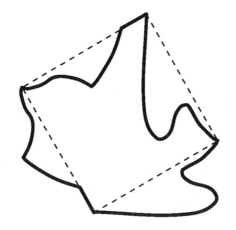

Paul O'Hearn

Grade: 12

Silver Lake Regional High School

Halifax, Massachusetts

Teacher: Phyliss Warren

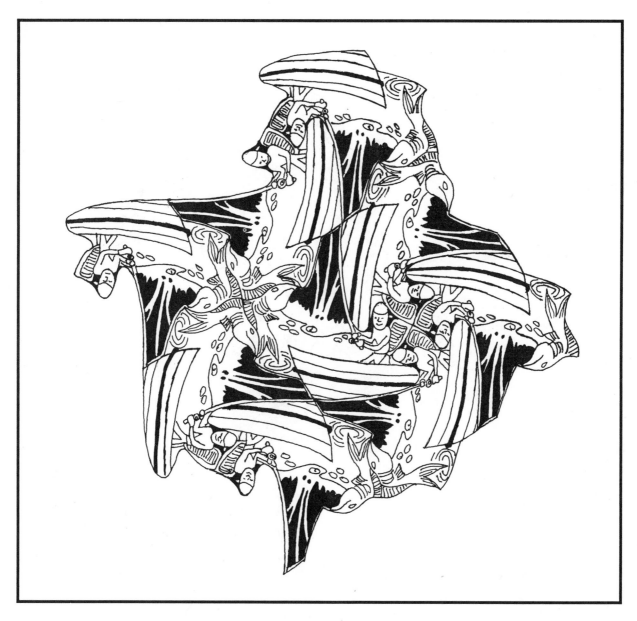

Todd Adamson

Grade: 11

Niceville High School

Niceville, Florida

Teacher: Mary Eplett

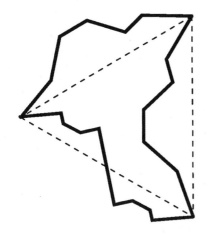

Robin Allred

Grade: Junior

Brigham Young University

Park City, Utah

Jonathan Bunch

Grade: 12

Marion High School

Marion, Illinois

Teacher: Catherine Howell

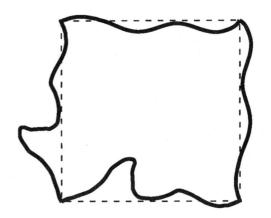

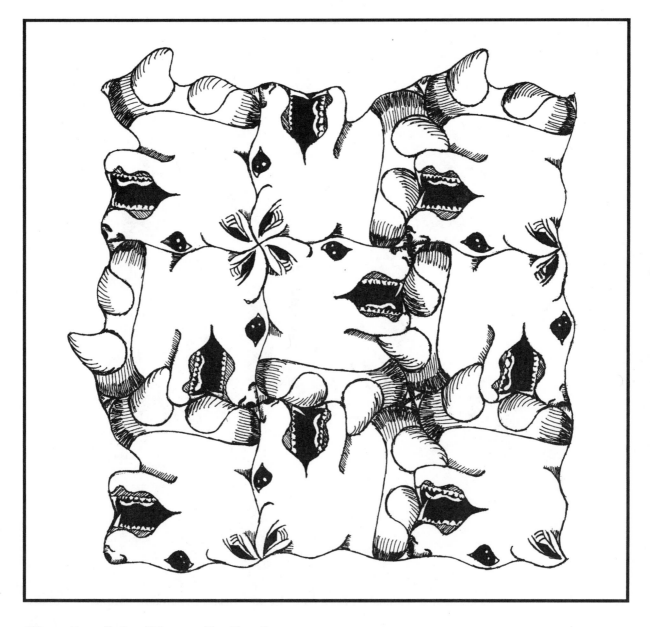

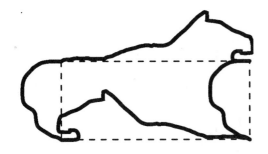

Amy B. Caldwell

Grade: 12

Tabb High School

Tabb, Virginia

Teacher: Faye M. Davis

Donnie Cook

Grade: 12

The Mississippi School for Math and Science

Columbus, Mississippi

Teacher: Claudia R. Carter

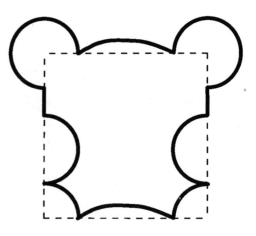

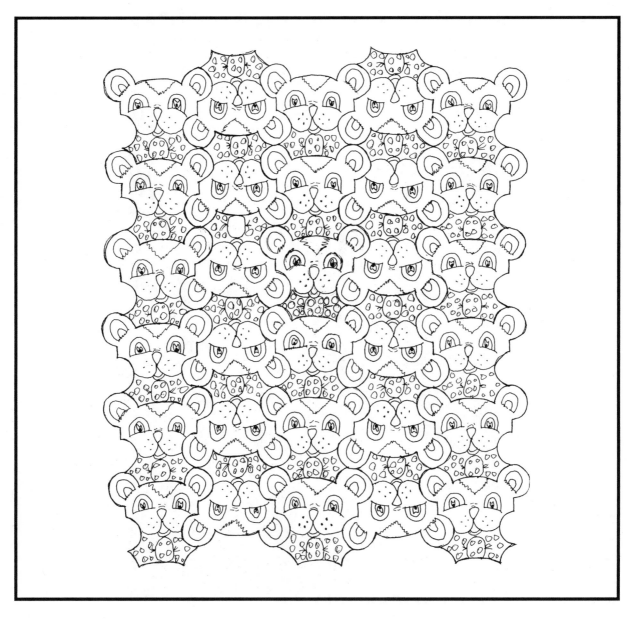

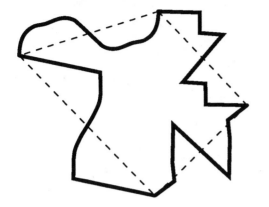

11–Up Honorable Mention

Tom Marcille

Grade: 11

Pinkerton Academy

Derry, New Hampshire

Teacher: Nancy Fletcher

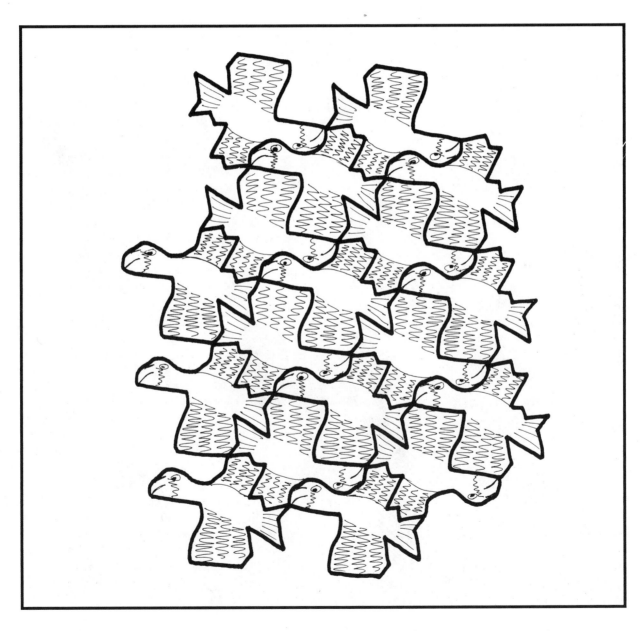

Edward R. Mears

Grade: 11

Pinkerton Academy

Derry, New Hampshire

Teacher: Nancy Fletcher

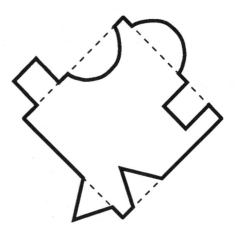

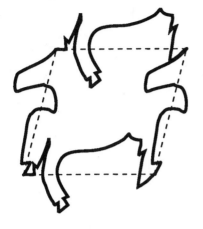

Britta Peterson

Grade: Sophomore

University of California, Davis

Davis, California

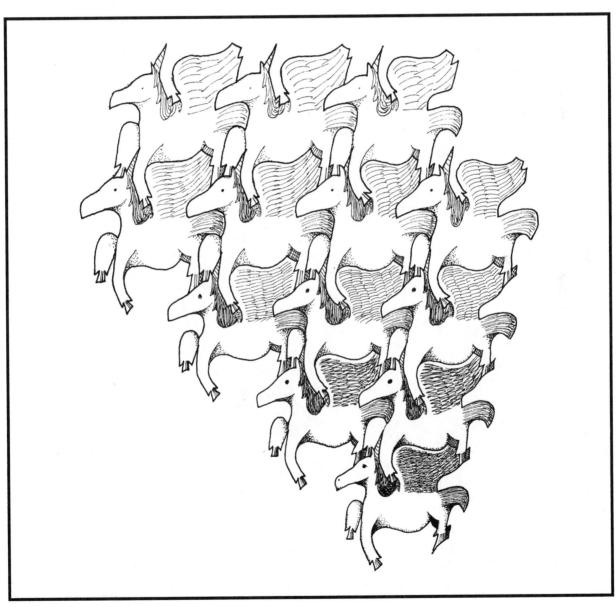

Steve Richmond

Grade: 12

Tabb High School

Tabb, Virginia

Teacher: Faye M. Davis

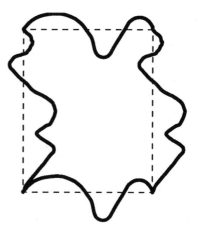

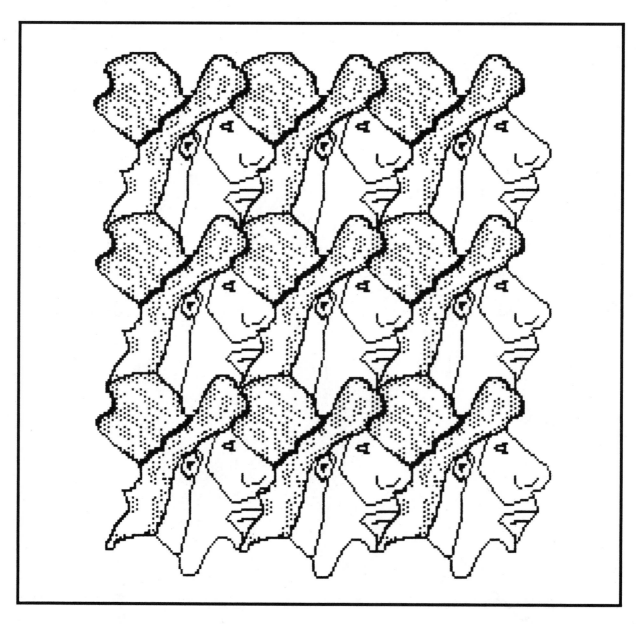

Steve Sawyer

Grade: 12

Marion High School

Marion, Illinois

Teacher: Catherine Howell

Derek Squire

Grade: 11

Lower Merion High School

Ardmore, Pennsylvania

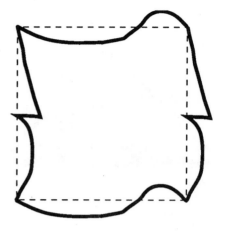

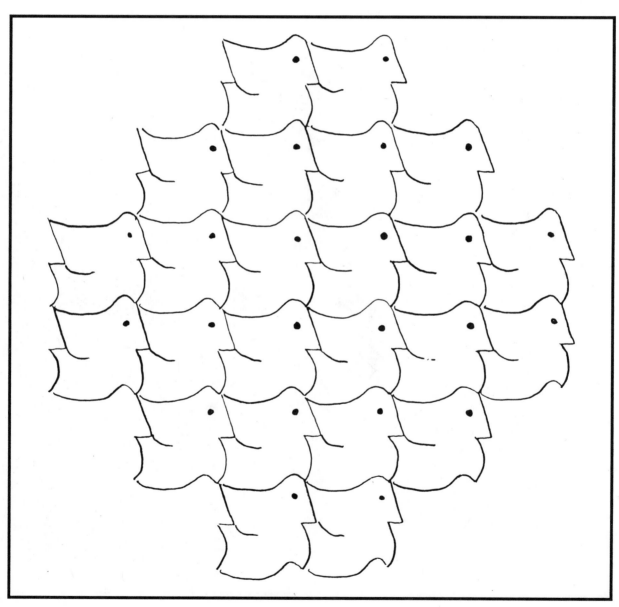

Overview of Tessellation Techniques

This overview is adapted from *Introduction to Tessellations* by Dale Seymour and Jill Britton (Palo Alto, CA: Dale Seymour Publications, 1989). For more details, please refer to that book.

Dutch graphic artist Maurits Cornelis Escher (1898–1972) created many perplexing tessellations. His preoccupation with tessellations developed after a 1936 visit to the Alhambra in Granada, Spain, an old Moorish palace decorated with mosaics in geometric patterns. Unlike the Moors, Escher did not restrict himself to abstract geometrical designs. Instead, he restricted himself to animate forms like the lizard we see in *Reptiles*, crawling out of Escher's two-dimensional sketch to explore the real world before rejoining his fellow reptiles in the interlocking design.

Reptiles by M. C. Escher (© 1990 M. C. Escher Heirs/Cordon Art, Baarn, Holland)

Escher's designs were plane tessellations. We define a tessellation of the plane as a pattern of shapes that fills the plane without any gaps or overlaps. The basis for any tessellating pattern is a grid of polygons—either triangles, quadrilaterals, or hexagons. Any triangle or quadrilateral will tessellate the plane. In addition, any hexagon whose opposite sides are parallel and congruent will tessellate. Examples of these tessellating grids are shown below.

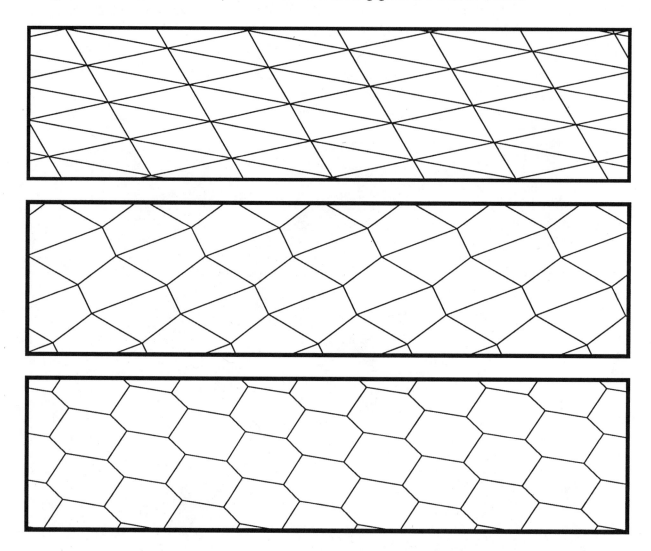

Various techniques can be used to transform triangles, quadrilaterals, or hexagons into animate shapes that tessellate the plane. These techniques involve transformations that we call translation, rotation, and reflection. The following pages give a brief summary of these techniques, some used by student contest winners in creating their Escher-like drawings.

Modifying Polygons by Translation

One way to create a tessellation design is to modify two sides of a parallelogram and translate those modifications to the opposite sides. A translation of a shape is a slide of that shape without rotation. The tessellating shape below is based on a square. The modification on side 1 is translated to side 3, and the modification on side 2 is translated to side 4.

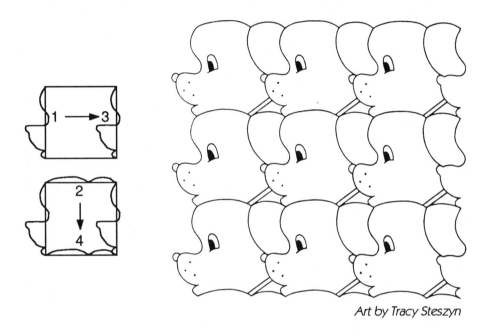

Art by Tracy Steszyn

The example below demonstrates the result when we modify a parallelogram by translation. Adding details to the interior of the shape makes it more interesting.

Art by Steve Dawson

Tessellation Winners: The First Contest   **81**

We can extend this method to include regular hexagons or, more generally, any hexagon having parallel and congruent sides. In hexagonal tessellations we have three sets of opposite sides to be modified. The following diagram demonstrates modifying a regular hexagon by translation. The tessellation, with details added, is shown below.

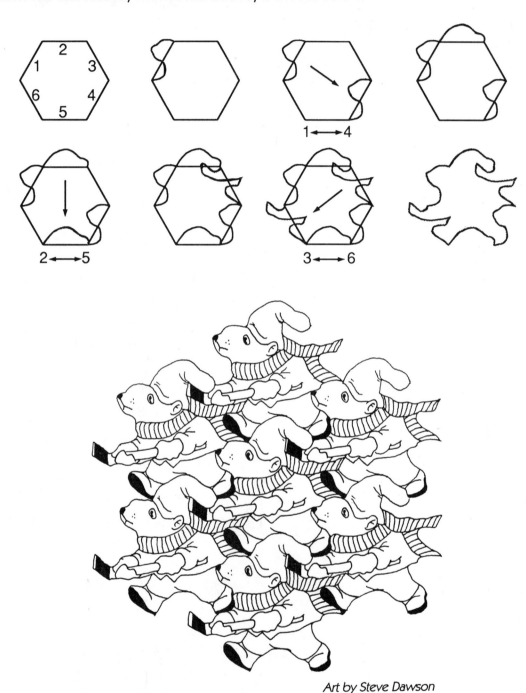

Art by Steve Dawson

Modifying Polygons by Rotation about Midpoints of Sides

Any quadrilateral will tessellate. Given the enormous variety of quadrilaterals available to us, we can use rotation about midpoints of sides to create a wealth of Escher-like tessellating shapes. The examples below are based on a square and a scalene quadrilateral, each modified by rotation about midpoints of sides.

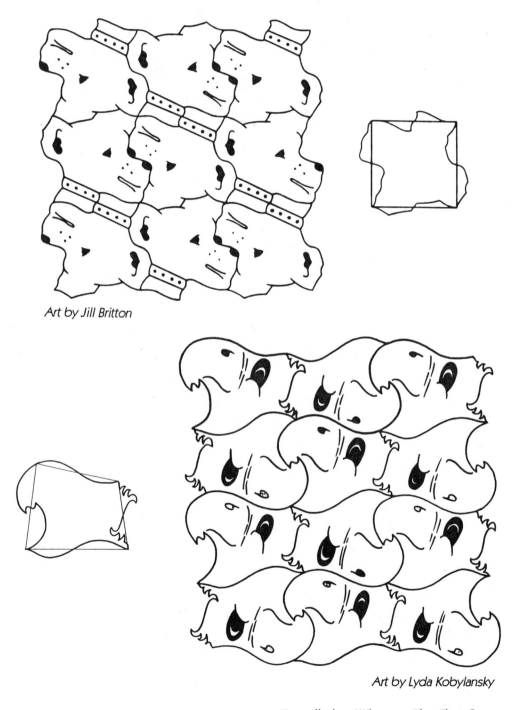

Art by Jill Britton

Art by Lyda Kobylansky

Art by Lyda Kobylansky

The example above shows a trapezoid modified by rotation about midpoints of sides. This same procedure works with any triangle. The below shape was created by modifying each half-side of a triangle and rotating the modification about the midpoint of the side.

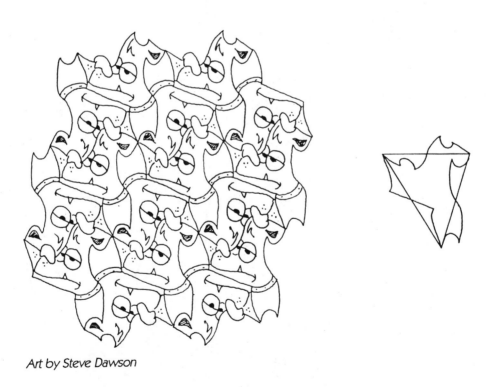

Art by Steve Dawson

Modifying Polygons by Translation and Rotation

The following diagram shows a rectangle modified by a combination of translation and rotation modifications. First, a modification is translated between the parallel congruent sides 2 and 4. Sides 1 and 3 are then transformed by a rotation of a modification about their midpoints.

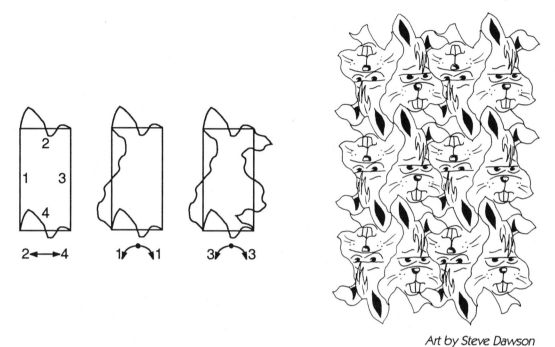

Art by Steve Dawson

Modifying Polygons by Rotation about Vertices

Using another technique, the square below has been modified by rotating side 1 to side 2 and side 3 to side 4. To use this technique, the adjacent sides must be congruent. In this case, we are rotating about a vertex of the polygon, not the midpoint of a side.

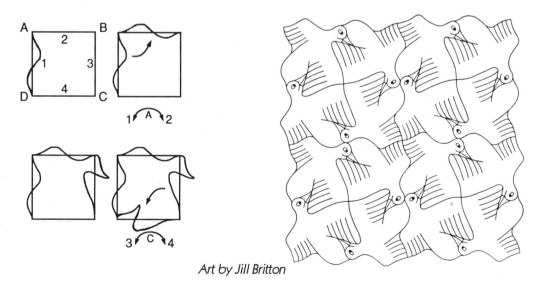

Art by Jill Britton

We can also create a tessellating shape by modifying a regular hexagon by rotation about vertices. In the example below, the resulting outline resembles a peg-legged pirate, even before we add interior details.

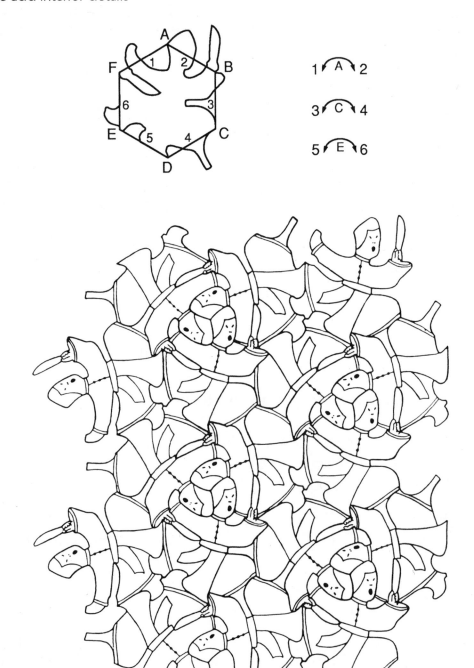

Art by Jill Britton

If we start with an equilateral or isosceles triangle we can use this technique with two of the sides, rotating a modification about the vertex. To avoid being stuck with the third side as a straight line, we can modify half of this third side and rotate about the midpoint to create a tessellating shape. The design below demonstrates this technique.

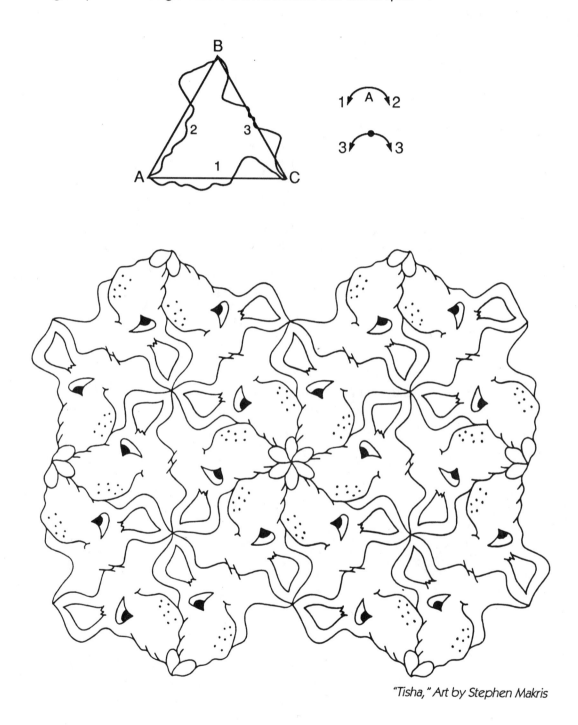

"Tisha," Art by Stephen Makris

Modifying Polygons by Reflection

Modification of tessellating polygons by reflection needs to involve either rotation or translation as well. An example that combines rotation and reflection in a special 120° isosceles triangle is shown below. Notice that the triangle is modified first by rotation at the vertex angle, then reflected to form a quadrilateral-based shape of a clown face with reflective symmetry.

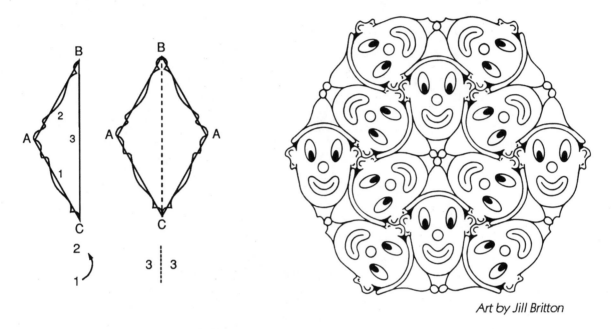

Art by Jill Britton

An example that combines reflection with translation is shown below. Side 1 is translated to side 3. The modification of side 4 is first reflected about a perpendicular line passing through the center of the parallelogram. Then that reflection is translated to side 2.

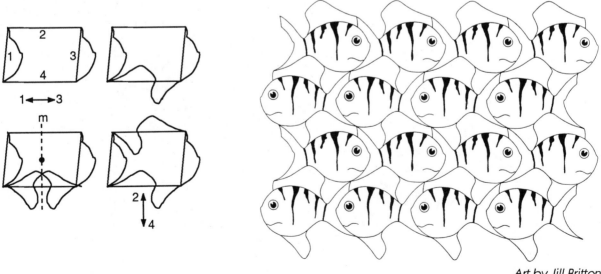

Art by Jill Britton

Imagination

It is helpful to have a good imagination when creating animated shapes. Certainly Escher had a great imagination. So did the student who saw at least six different images in the shape below, which he created by rotation modifications.

duck

bird

mutant horse

goblin

dragon

cuckoo

Art by Steve Dawson

Tips for Beginners

Designing an Escher-like shape and drawing its tessellation is a time-consuming yet satisfying exercise. Following are some practical tips to help you get started.

A scalene quadrilateral allows you the greatest freedom and flexibility when you attempt your first design. However long its sides and whatever the size of its angles, a quadrilateral will tessellate the plane. If half of each of the sides is modified and the modifications are rotated 180° about their midpoints, the resulting shape will also tessellate the plane.

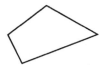   

| Step 1. Draw a scalene quadrilateral | Step 2. Modify half of any side | Step 3. Rotate modified line 180 degrees | Step 4. Repeat procedure with other 3 sides |

Once your preliminary sketch is completed, you must prepare an accurate version of the shape for your tessellation. One simple and practical approach is to cut the original polygon shape from construction paper or lightweight cardboard, then cut appropriate "holes" and tape them on as corresponding "bumps" to represent your modifications. (In the case of glide reflection, you will need to flip the bump before taping.)

To create the tessellation, position your pattern on another sheet of paper, trace about its perimeter, and mark the location of interior details. By repositioning and tracing the pattern again and again, you will see the tessellation evolve before your eyes.

A more precise procedure involves no cutting and allows you more freedom in adding interior details—but it also requires more time and patience, and either a light table or a window that you can draw against. You will need three sheets of translucent paper. Draw your polygon on two of these. Then, on one polygon, draw your modifications to the sides in *one* of their two locations. Tape this polygon to a window or light table and superimpose the second polygon precisely on top. Trace your initial modifications, then move the superimposed sheet as needed to locate and trace each modification in its new location. You end up with an accurately drawn shape to serve as your pattern, to which you can add interior details at will.

Now you need to create the underlying grid for your tessellating polygon. To avoid the problem of grid lines in your finished design, we suggest drawing the *mirror image* of the grid on the *back* of the third sheet of translucent paper. That way, when you tape this sheet face up over your pattern at the window or light table, you can see the grid lines to help you position your shape, but they will not appear in your final drawing. (Alternatively, of course, you could draw the grid on a separate sheet and draw your final design on yet another sheet placed over it—but three sheets of paper overlaid are fairly opaque, even with a light table.)

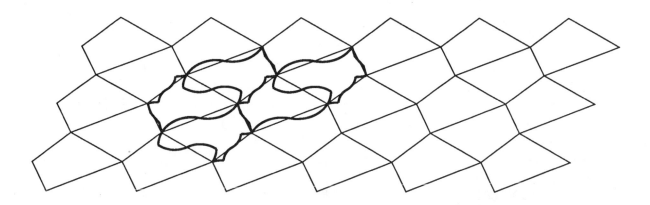

From here on, completing the drawing is simply a matter of meticulous tracing. You align a polygon in the grid precisely with the polygon of your pattern, then trace all marks except the polygon on the top sheet. Select an adjacent polygon, turn the sheet to align with the pattern, and trace—continuing in this manner until you are satisfied with the extent of your tessellation.

Resources: Teaching Tessellation Techniques

Bezuszka, S., M. Kenney, and L. Silvey. 1978, 1990. *Designs from Mathematical Patterns.* Palo Alto, CA: Dale Seymour Publications.
Explores the application of mathematics to design, with activities that relate number patterns to tessellations. Grade 6 to adult. 208 pp.

———. 1977. *Tessellations: The Geometry of Patterns.* Palo Alto, CA: Creative Publications.
Elementary lessons and practice exercises involving basic tessellations. Grade 5 to adult. 170 pp.

Kenney, M. and S. Bezuszka. 1987. *Tessellations Using Logo.* Palo Alto, CA: Dale Seymour Publications.
Collection of 71 activities using Terrapin Logo as a tool for sketching simple and complex tessellations, including Escher-like tessellations. Grade 7 to adult. 96 pp.

Oliver, J. 1979. *Polysymetrics.* Norfolk, England: Tarquin Publications.
Tips on creating simple and complex geometric tilings, with faint-line grids for drawing original patterns. Grade 7 to adult. 40 pp.

Ranucci, E. R., and J. L. Teeters. 1977. *Creating Escher-Type Drawings.* Palo Alto, CA: Creative Publications.
A how-to book presenting the principles of plane tessellations, symmetry, and the transformations used to create Escher-type designs, with worksheets and grids for practicing the techniques presented. Includes a chapter on analyzing Escher's tessellations. Grade 6 to adult. 200 pp.

Seymour, D. 1989. *Tessellation Teaching Masters.* Palo Alto, CA: Dale Seymour Publications.
A resource for teacher or student, with full-page designs suitable for transparencies or worksheets. Includes tessellations of regular and nonregular polygons; semiregular tessellations; patterns with star polygons, polyominoes, letters, and nonpolygonal shapes; designs based on duals; and Islamic art. With sketching grids and templates to aid in drawing new designs. Grade 6 to adult. 288 pp.

Seymour, D. and J. Britton. 1989. *Introduction to Tessellations.* Palo Alto, CA: Dale Seymour Publications.
A comprehensive, easy-to-read resource book that explores the fundamental concepts of tessellations, including procedures for creating Escher-like designs. Key topics, supported by hundreds of graphic illustrations, include properties of tessellations, regular and semi-regular tessellations, symmetry and transformations, techniques for generating tessellations, Islamic art, and Escher tessellations. Grade 6 to adult. 264 pp.

Resources: The Art of M. C. Escher

Bool, F. H., J. R. Kist, J. L. Locher, and F. Wierda. 1981. *M. C. Escher: His Life and Complete Graphic Work.* New York: Harry N. Abrams, Inc.
A detailed biography and complete record of Escher's graphic art. Contains a comprehensive catalog of his works, with descriptions and additional information about some 450 prints that are largely unknown or rarely reproduced. 600 illustrations. Grade 7 to adult. 354 pp.

Coxeter, H. S. M., M. Emmer, R. Penrose, and M. L. Teuber. 1986. *M. C. Escher: Art and Science.* New York: Elsevier Science Publishing Co., Inc.
Articles from the proceedings of an interdisciplinary congress devoted to Escher's work and its relationship to mathematics (including symmetry and geometry), computer graphics, art, science, and the humanities. Grade 10 to adult. 404 pp.

Ernst, B. 1985. *The Magic Mirror of M. C. Escher.* Norfolk: Tarquin Publications.
A detailed description of the conception and execution of Escher's most popular prints, with sketches and diagrams showing how the artist arrived at his astonishing creations. Grade 7 to adult. 116 pp.

Escher, M. C. 1971. *The World of M. C. Escher.* New York: Harry N. Abrams, Inc.
A comprehensive survey of Escher's work. Includes 300 sketches and prints, Escher's essay "Approaches to Infinity," several articles about his work, and a catalog listing of prints. Grade 7 to adult. 268 pp.

———. 1967. *The Graphic Work of M. C. Escher.* New York: Ballantine Books.
Seventy-six of Escher's designs classified into nine categories to represent concepts such as mirror images (reflections) and divisions of a plane (tessellations). Introduced and explained by the artist. Grade 7 to adult. 96 pp.

MacGillavry, C. 1976. *Fantasy and Symmetry: The Periodic Drawings of M. C. Escher.* New York: Harry N. Abrams, Inc.
An exploration of the laws underlying different types of tessellations, with 41 of Escher's prints and drawings. 84 pp.

Schattschneider, D. 1990. *Visions of Symmetry: Notebooks, Periodic Drawings, and Related Work of M. C. Escher.* New York: W. H. Freeman and Company.
A comprehensive book that illustrates Escher's passion for symmetry and traces the development of his tessellations. Contains two Escher Notebooks (1941–1942), sketches, letters, and diary entries. Includes over 350 illustrations, including 180 never previously published. Grade 10 to adult. 354 pp.

Filling a plane with a pattern, without gaps and without overlaps . . .

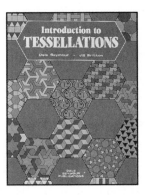

Introduction to Tessellations
by Dale Seymour and Jill Britton
264 pages

A clear, understandable introduction to tessellations and other intriguing geometric designs. Written for teachers of grades 6–12, this complete resource contains hundreds of fascinating examples that explore:

- polygons
- regular polygons and combinations of regular polygons
- Escher-type tessellations
- Islamic art designs
- tessellating letters
    . . . and much more

Order number DS07901

Tessellation Teaching Masters
by Dale Seymour
288 pages

This companion book to *Introduction to Tessellations* contains more than 270 full-page tessellating design patterns. Reproduce them to give students practice creating their own patterns or to use as overhead transparencies.

Order number DS07900

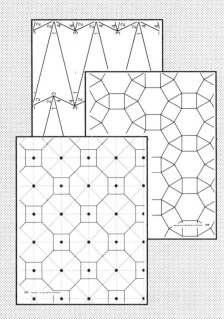

1-800-872-1100

Geometric Concepts in Islamic Art
by Issam El-Said and Ayse Parman
176 pages

A fascinating pictorial explanation of how Islamic art is based on geometric patterns. Photographs of mausoleums, minarets, and other objects are followed by corresponding diagrams that start with the circle and divide it into elaborate star-shaped polygons. Written for grades 10 and up.

Order number DS07803

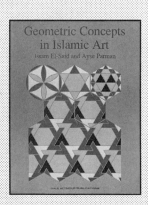

Geometric Concepts in Islamic Art
Issam El-Said and Ayse Parman

Students and Teachers:

Enter Our Second

ESCHER-LIKE ART CONTEST

Win Dale Seymour Publications Merchandise

See Your Tessellation in Print!

Winners will receive a copy of a book featuring the winning designs, as well as a copy of *Introduction to Tessellations* by Dale Seymour and Jill Britton. The top winners will also receive a $50 gift certificate for merchandise carried by Dale Seymour Publications.

Contest Rules on Reverse

Contest Rules

Sample Entry

1. Each entry must be submitted on two sheets of unlined 8½-by-11-inch white paper.

2. On the first sheet, draw the generating polygon with modifying curves superimposed in their appropriate locations. Modifying curves may be transformed by any of these procedures: translation, rotation, reflection, and glide reflection. The resulting shape should not exceed 3 inches in diameter in any direction. Do not show added details on this first sheet.

3. On the second sheet, show the completed tessellation with interior details added. Make all markings with black ink, lead pencil, or a computer printer. Do not use color or pencil shading.

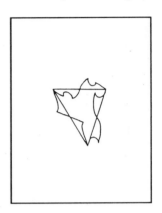

4. All drawings must be the original work of a teacher or of a student enrolled in one of the grades K–12 or college on the submission date.

5. Computer-generated entries will be judged separately from hand-drawn designs.

6. Mail entries, **along with a completed entry form,** by June 30, 1992, to ESCHER-LIKE ART CONTEST, Dale Seymour Publications, P.O. Box 10888, Palo Alto, CA 94303. Keep a copy of the submitted artwork.

7. By submitting your artwork, you agree that all rights in that artwork, including all copyrights, are assigned to and become the property of Dale Seymour Publications, and shall be considered "work made for hire" under the copyright act. Entries cannot be returned.

8. For a list of winners, send a self-addressed stamped envelope, Attention: Tessellation Contest Winners, after October 1, 1992.

- -

Entry Form

Name _____

Grade_____ (the grade you are now in or have most recently completed)

School_____ Teacher_____

School Address _____

Home Address _____

I verify that this is my original artwork, and I understand that it will become the property of Dale Seymour Publications as a "work made for hire" under the copyright act.

Signature_____

Parent's Signature _____
    (student and parent or guardian must both sign for students under 18 years of age)

For teachers of students submitting artwork: I give permission for my name to accompany this ˙dent's artwork if it appears in forthcoming Dale Seymour Publications material.

        's Signature _____